D0491182

BLISS

DEBS CARLING

BALBOA.
PRESS
A DIVISION OF HAY HOUSE

Copyright © 2018 Debs Carling.

All rights reserved. No part of this book may be used or reproduced by any means, graphic, electronic, or mechanical, including photocopying, recording, taping or by any information storage retrieval system without the written permission of the author except in the case of brief quotations embodied in critical articles and reviews.

Balboa Press books may be ordered through booksellers or by contacting:

Balboa Press
A Division of Hay House
1663 Liberty Drive
Bloomington, IN 47403
www.balboapress.com.au
1 (877) 407-4847

Because of the dynamic nature of the Internet, any web addresses or links contained in this book may have changed since publication and may no longer be valid. The views expressed in this work are solely those of the author and do not necessarily reflect the views of the publisher, and the publisher hereby disclaims any responsibility for them.

The author of this book does not dispense medical advice or prescribe the use of any technique as a form of treatment for physical, emotional, or medical problems without the advice of a physician, either directly or indirectly. The intent of the author is only to offer information of a general nature to help you in your quest for emotional and spiritual well-being. In the event you use any of the information in this book for yourself, which is your constitutional right, the author and the publisher assume no responsibility for your actions.

Any people depicted in stock imagery provided by Getty Images are models, and such images are being used for illustrative purposes only.
Certain stock imagery © Getty Images.

Print information available on the last page.

ISBN: 978-1-5043-1466-4 (sc)
ISBN: 978-1-5043-1469-5 (e)

Balboa Press rev. date: 10/12/2018

Dedicated to Jan Carling who moves freely
now as part of consciousness whole.

CONTENTS

Purpose 1

Answers 3

Choices 5

Access From Within 7

Close Your Eyes 9

Higher Consciousness 11

Cosmic Documentary 13

Accessing Source-Part 1 15

Accessing Source-Part 2 17

Access To The Divine 19

CHAnge 21

Celestial Parental Advice 23

I Am That I Am- I Am Nameless 25

Footprints In The Sand 27

Kundalini 29

Meditation 31

Silent Communication 33

Guilt 35

A Shared Journey 37

Mother Nature 39

Unrealised Potential 41

Your Heart's Song 43

Mean Average 45

Atom 47

Mighty Star 49

Human Suit 51

Brain 53

Aura Energy 55

Koi Carp 57

Man's Nagging Doubt... 59

Harbour Master 61

Spiritual Junkies... 63

Space-Part 1 65

Space-Part 2 67

Finding Within-Part 1 69

Finding Within-Part 2 71

Expectations... 73

Forever Present... 75

Lemongrass 77

A Dog's Understanding... 79

Familiar Strangers 81

Ego 83

A Cow Living In The Now 85

Mosquito.. 87

Lady On The Beach 89

Perspective 91

Safe Holding 93

Flip Flop 95

Ants On A Rope 97

The

PURPOSE

What is our purpose,
Why are we here,
To experience love,
And learn from our fear.

To shut off the noise,
And open heart wide,
To live life fully, with
Inner love recognised.

To utilise intuition,
Align with life's flow,
A shift from a question,
To a place where we know.

Universe

ANSWERS

For years now you so long,
Answers on the edge of your tongue,
Information niggling to be free,
Stirs inside your cell memory.

Then suddenly you just know,
Your intuition tells you so,
Source energy becomes immense,
It erupts from you with providence.

Life now filled with creative flare,
Inspiration comes from everywhere,
A higher vibration once suppressed,
Wakes up like a hornet's nest.

A spiritual wind has found your sail,
Confidence replaces the fear to fail,
A recollection of facts within you,
A resurgence of answers you always knew.

hears

CHOICES

I choose to believe,
Source power exists, and
Our choices and actions
Add energy to this mix.

I choose to believe,
Our knowledge is lacking,
That the Universe is simply,
Beyond our formatting.

I choose to believe,
All outcomes are fine,
We gain much through them,
All factored in our design.

I choose to believe,
In my own intuition,
It will point out a path,
Reveal my life's mission.

I choose to believe,
The right teacher arrives,
When we are ready,
To open our eyes.

I choose to believe,
Prophets and messengers,
Are sent to impart,
Information to listeners.

I choose to believe,
That cosmic inspiration,
Comes to us if we
Send out the invitation.

you,

ACCESS FROM WITHIN

Suppose if there was no time,
No framework for a future or past,
Challenged the might of Einstein,
A space incomprehensibly vast.

An existence with laws of physics,
So alien not even an atom,
Folds and twists and an unknown mix,
Well beyond all our studies and datum.

Quantum mysteries too complex for,
A large Hadron Collider to break in,
Other dimensional layers for sure,
But only accessible to us from within.

Your

CLOSE YOUR EYES

Close your eyes in order to perceive,
The critical faculty of your inner senses,
Receptor nerves can detect outside molecules,
Even the viscosity of the air that suspends us.

You can also identify the volume,
Of a body of water located nearby,
If you detach from cues you've deciphered,
Using information obtained through your eye.

Test yourself by detecting layers of wildlife,
Active in the air and the ground all around you,
Feel the palpable essence of the life force,
In the trees and the grass that surrounds you.

Become sensitive to nature's delicate surges,
An eyes-closed acute awareness of being,
A discerning interpreting of the information,
Which open eyes are incapable of seeing.

Sit quietly and close your eyes completely,
Disregard what your brain is saying,
Just connect with the vibrations and energy,
Of what the planet is actually relaying

questions

HIGHER CONSCIOUSNESS

I sense you,
I know you're there,
I feel your presence,
Like wind in my hair.

The more I trust,
Lay myself bare,
The more of you,
I am aware.

get

COSMIC DOCUMENTARY

Think about what's on TV,
So full of negativity,
Dictating how we think and see,
Reducing our productivity.

It's turned on for hours on end,
A boring, draining familiar friend,
A drug on which we depend,
Sucks us in a life condemned.

We convince ourself it's education,
An 'open university for the nation',
But we are giving our brain away,
A willing participant of its decay.

Instead look up at the stars,
At the Cosmic Universe memoirs,
A source of enriching variety,
A real life documentary.

Infinite interest for everyone,
Drama, tension, passion, song,
Comedy, life, death and sci-fi,
And eternity to be consumed by.

To those so inquisitively inclined,
An open invitation to free their mind,
Answers to every question in waiting,
The 'big unknown', truly captivating.

through,

ACCESSING SOURCE-PART 1

You have a magical hidden feature,
Using your inherent
attraction to nature,
You can connect to
another dimension,
We all have that knowledge
and inclination.

The frequency for this
easy to find, but
Only achieved during
quietness of mind,
Release all thoughts
away in a balloon,
As calm spreads you'll
start to attune.

When you invite Source Energy in,
It waits for permission
before entering,
Then you will feel it
filling you like a cup,
Into your toes then all the way up.

As your breathing intensity slows,
The Cosmic layers will
begin to show,
This is where your trust
must come in,
Ego will distract you with
a loud beckoning.

Firmly and kindly tell
your ego to go,
It will dutifully retreat, it will know,
Cosmic connection can
now be accessed,
Your spiritual essence no
longer suppressed.

Feel your soul's eagerness to be free,
Re-uniting with other
souls in Divinity,
Escaping confinement
enjoying the unravel,
Dancing at high velocity
in astro-travel.

Learn to meditate, each
day a little longer,
You will feel your connection
getting stronger,
Stay in tune with nature's heartbeat,
Aligned with Source you'll
start feeling complete.

Sometimes meditation
can be a simple affair,
The sun on your face or
the wind in your hair,
Just five minutes whenever
you're able to,
An empowering development
of your own inner guru.

What

ACCESSING SOURCE-PART 2
continued

Other times you will be
drawn to longer sessions,
Sunrise and sunset times for
powerful meditations,
A conscious engagement
in real mindfulness,
Escaping life's streaming
dialogue and busyness.

The Source is energy
always within reach,
It wants to help us and
be accessed to teach,
But we must utilize our free
will and ask it to show,
Meditation sets the scene, shows
intent and lets it know.

you

ACCESS TO THE DIVINE

I've been to a place,
Revealed to me of
Unimaginable beauty,
Meditation took me there,
It showed to me the subtle stair.

A silencing of the chatter,
Unveiled to me a shrine,
A new space and time,
An open invitation,
To the Divine.

seek

CHAnge

Such tenuous beliefs and foul epithets,
Believes in nothing, except conveniently so,
Sits on the fence, a hedging of bets,
No backbone that ever dares show.

Flits from one thing to another,
"I'll do that forever, in a minute",
A longing inside for he knows he'd rather,
Find life's meaning and immerse within it.

Suddenly, change he never saw coming,
He's consumed with an urge to sing, and
An inexplicable desire to start writing,
Creative passion rising inside of him.

Bombarded by inspiration flooding in,
Some external power is filtering it in,
He can't put a name to the provider, but
Is now a committed life-long subscriber.

A disappearance of rages burning,
Inner turmoil exchanged for such calm,
His profanity replaced by sweet humming,
A gentle demeanor and even a charm.

His face appears softer and kinder,
Great pride from what he's achieving,
The coarse themes of his tattoos a reminder,
Of the years of self-doubt and disbelieving.

seeks

CELESTIAL PARENTAL ADVICE

I encourage you to live your life,
Steered by your internal voices,
To set your own moral compass,
Using your free will and choices.

Let your values sincerely guide you,
In sync with your miraculous heart,
And improve the world a little bit,
By cultivating kindness as your art.

Spread your inner goodness,
And be unique though as you do it,
For you are an infinitely shining star,
With a potential that has no limit.

you

I AM THAT I AM- I AM NAMELESS

The Tao Te Ching teaching is strong,
Regarding the naming of anything as quite wrong,
Such defining restricts one's full perception,
A label is limiting, without exception.

Try viewing familiar objects as nameless things,
That's neither a bird nor those are his wings,
He is '*colourful, organic, beautiful grace,*
Miraculously synchronised cells in air space.

A collection of atoms held within fleshy skin,
A perfect combination and order though within,
A dance of electrical impulses and energy,
A precise chemical and biological alchemy.'

Apply this and see everything as nameless,
View every object in the world eyes afresh,
It's startling how one's perspective is changed,
Illustrates how perfectly everything is arranged.

too,

FOOTPRINTS IN THE SAND

Footprints in the sand at night,
Empty beach in the moonlight,
There's indentations of who was here,
The people are gone but still feel near.

I place my foot into another's print,
And feel them just the slightest hint,
Then many more I trace and glide,
I guess their weight, their gait and stride.

An exchange of energy is occurring,
As if the spirit world is stirring,
I'm accessing something on this beach,
A residue of auras within my reach.

I wonder how much we're not seeing,
Limited awareness of a human being.
This mystifying experience has revealed that,
Occasionally our worlds really do overlap.

I sometimes feel the Cosmos energy,
Knowledge of the Universe, so nearly,
It feels as if it's becoming clear,
But then the answers simply disappear.

Perhaps we are not designed to know,
We are here to simply learn and to grow,
To acknowledge what is perfect and destined,
A journey that's not meant to be questioned.

Quiet

KUNDALINI

Awakened dormant energy,
Very slowly consciously,
Expansion of serpent Shakti,
Raising Kundalini.

Fog replaced by clarity,
Chakras spinning freely,
Light shining internally,
Raising Kundalini.

Mind now thinking clearly,
Eyes no longer bleary,
Alertness replacing dreary,
Raising Kundalini.

Aura glows alluringly,
Strength grows increasingly,
A higher vibrational intensity,
The power of Kundalini.

your

MEDITATION

When I sit and meditate,
I have no thought and don't narrate,
I relax into a deep calm state,
A blissful floating I create.

A vibrational higher gear,
I tell my ego to disappear,
My soul expands with the all clear,
And we float into the atmosphere.

We enter the consciousness whole,
Astro-travelling with my soul,
Far beyond the celestial poles,
Another world through this keyhole.

A place that feels entirely free,
A restful timeless journey,
My eyes closed I'm an absentee,
A true meditation devotee.

mind

SILENT COMMUNICATION

Imagine communication without
Any speech or conversations,
Done through our thoughts and feelings,
A silent exchange of all emotions.

A simple translation of honesty,
No masking of facts or pretending to be,
What you feel comes across freely,
Emulating our pets use of telepathy.

Tapping into a raw primal insight,
With intuition the great driving energy,
Remembering the skills of long past,
Of our natural ability to perform ESP.

and

GUILT

So much hunger,
Lack of grain,
We all feel guilty,
For third world pain.

Impure water,
Millions wilt,
Mass suffering,
We all feel guilt.

Homeless guy,
We pat purse,
"No change" lie,
Our guilt gets worse.

We have plenty,
Living freely,
We feel our guilt,
So completely.

More focus,
On being kind,
Live guilt free,
And clear our mind.

With a stranger,
Share a smile,
Stop and chat,
For a while.

This small act
Of affection,
Done globally,
Is mass connection.

To exist with
Guilt removed,
Love thy neighbour,
Is the world improved.

it

A SHARED JOURNEY

Feel your soul
Grow each day,
Grows from birth,
Then we pass away.

Ashes to ashes,
No longer someone,
The soul still grows
When we're gone.

Enriched and nourished,
From human body,
Returns to Source,
Amorphous energy.

This spiritual essence
Again keen to return,
As a human form
Experience and learn.

A human life
Is not mundane,
A soul seeks it
Time and time again.

At times when choices
Have you off course,
Knowledge is gained,
Your soul does endorse.

The more you dare
Adventure multiplied,
Your soul will thrive
You'll feel satisfied.

Experience life fully,
Uniquely and joyfully,
Feel soul dancing
Within you playfully.

A soul chose you,
Co-joined at birth,
Enjoy this gift,
Your life on earth.

will

MOTHER NATURE

I place my feet right by the sea,
Shallow waves nudging up to me,
I love the reflection and the shine,
A spiritual moment every time.

Where the water meets the sand,
Is like viewing Mother Nature's hand,
Her finger tips reach for me,
And tickle my toes ever so gently.

A sea breeze flows with her tonight,
So alluring under the moonlight,
Wave rhythm emulating breathing,
An electric energy that I'm receiving.

In the sand she leaves her print,
As she retreats a subtle hint,
A dark ochre patch if you want to share,
Next wave in she'll meet you there.

Then after which you walk away,
To be re-united another day,
Always guaranteed to do the same,
Listen carefully, she'll whisper your name.

find

UNREALISED POTENTIAL

The average individual,
A clueless brilliant fool,
Holds unrealised potential,
And its unlocking tool.

For him to trigger this,
Awaken the power within,
All that's simply required is,
Conscious activation from him.

you.

YOUR HEART'S SONG

Do something
Every day,
Which makes your heart
Sing in every way.

There is no right,
There is no wrong,
As long as you follow,
Your heart's song.

All you need,
Is under the sun,
Available
To everyone.

It

MEAN AVERAGE

The gift of life,
Unique, none the same,
And yet so familiar to us,
It's become rather mundane.

A mean average formula,
Based on eighty years, or so,
A mindset of just surviving,
Listing problems as they grow.

No thought happening,
A defaulted autopilot,
An existence of complaining,
Just how little we have got.

Life is endured much,
Like long haul travel,
With slight irritation, like
Walking barefoot on gravel.

Just living for work,
Putting on hold any fun,
Wishing time away waiting
For retirement to come.

So busy and blinkered,
Consumed with the rat race,
Bored and discontented,
Blind to life's grace.

Eventually the question,
Why are we here?
Is there greater purpose than
Social status and career?

For some it's grasped early,
They see magic in the light,
Comes so easily to them,
A natural flow and insight.

For others, it takes them,
Until their moment of death,
The mystery makes sense,
During their final breath.

We do all gain clarity of,
Our spectacular human worth,
The experience and the growth,
From our time here on earth.

But to maximise this potential,
To walk the planet fully awake,
The sooner we spiritually awaken,
The more progress we can make.

will

ATOM

A pin head is so very small,
Upon its point so miniscule,
Five million-million atoms all,
Packed in tightly wall to wall.

The Cosmos is so very immense,
The atmosphere much less dense,
An atom per centimeter there,
A colossal space with really thin air.

flow

MIGHTY STAR

In between clouds,
Sits a star shining bright,
On its own, but
Giving off intense light.

It seems to be glowing
With all of its might,
Projecting luminosity,
A vast distance tonight.

A ray travelling,
Many light years it covers,
The distance from us over
Forty trillion kilometers.

Four years to reach us,
A massive journey to embark,
A four trillion year life cycle,
Which burns out and goes dark.

Information amassed,
Within its beautiful beam,
All the Cosmos secrets,
It has gathered and seen.

A continuous live streaming,
Of its story so far,
A light show spectacular,
Of this mighty little star.

in

HUMAN SUIT

We are all spinning orbs of
energy, light and love,
Wearing a human suit, squeezed
in tightly like a glove,
Each orb comes from the one-
ness, separated as a spark,
A benevolent loving energy
linked to our heart.

We identify ourself as the
suit driven by its brain,
We attach importance to the
appearance of its frame,
Occasionally though, we hear
our heart call and sing,
And feel its love and
sense of all knowing.

Yet for decades our suit and
its brain run the show,
It makes all the decisions for
us, as if it's in the know,
The orb lets this happen and
quite enjoys the ride,
Colourfully spinning away
linked to our chakras inside.

Intuition takes over and the
orb becomes prominent,
Our choices act as a trigger
for it to now be dominant,

Our spiritual essence is
wanting to be remembered,
The brain/suit power becomes
somewhat tempered.

The orb starts to make itself
known, shining bright,
We find inner love and an
attraction to the light,
We feel our real truth and
start aligning with nature,
We start to question who we
are, who's our creator?

We feel an expansion as our
orb yearns to be free,
The zip of our suit loosens
and we sing joyfully,
We realise we are our orb, the
spark of all that is one,
It seems so obvious now, we
should have known all along.

A journey near completion is
now being led by our heart,
A Divine vibrational energy we
have carried from the start,
The human life experience now
has run its natural course,
In death we shed the suit and
reunite back with Source.

quiet

BRAIN

What is a cerebrum,
Aqueous viscous jelly,
But how miraculous,
Such functionality.

Its signaling neurons
Amount to billions,
Synapses link them
In their trillions.

Dendrites and axons
Information exchange,
Abundance under the
Meninges membrane.

Sixty percent fat, and
Seventy-five water,
Solver of problems,
Information sorter.

A reducer valve,
For consciousness in,
Cosmic messages,
Constantly filtering.

To capture what is
Spiritually fruitful,
Put your brain
Right into neutral.

and

AURA ENERGY

Energy and light constitutes what is all,
Every oscillating vibrating molecule,
Each physical body is ever so subtly,
Surrounded by an electromagnetic energy.

It has a translucent colourful presence,
We're aware of it with an intuitive sense,
This force is referred to as aura energy,
We react to each other's quite subconsciously.

It whispers to us with a silent communication,
It is part of the powerful law of attraction,
A room of strangers we are compelled to know,
Anyone with a similar energy flow.

Auras are formed by our thoughts and actions,
Our intentions, body language, words and reactions,
A force that once released travels for eternity,
And incorporates into the one-ness energy.

What we feel and think is our silent truth,
Shimmering from us like heat off a tin roof,
If a person is joyful, or even heavy and tense,
We feel this in the air with a palpable essence.

Misery or negativity is a very real projection,
Soon a pandemic, spread much like an infection,
Thus we all hold the responsibility to be more positive,
And release into the world a more harmonious narrative.

curious,

KOI CARP

A koi carp swimming in a lake,
Gliding smoothly leaving no wake,
A centred energy and a calm existence,
A serene place that makes perfect sense.

The carp is stillness and in no hurry,
No actual comprehension of worry,
A man stares down from a bridge above,
Equipped to think, to feel, and love.

But there he stands, eyes cast down,
Upon his face a sad dark frown,
All that thinking has done for him,
Is to cause doubt and make him question.

The carp's energy travels beyond border,
Through the layer where the air meets the water,
It enters the man with invisible grace,
Lifting the sadness and frown from his face.

The act of being to the carp so natural,
He moves with ease, so equilateral,
The man stands tall, so much stronger,
Feels his own flow, depressed no longer.

As quick as that the decision is made,
A flick of a switch and no longer afraid,
The man strides off energised once again, and
The carp glides away with the ease that he came.

A

MAN'S NAGGING DOUBT

I doubt that I am good enough,
I doubt that all is fine,
I doubt that I can even make
A simple poem rhyme.

I doubt that I am clever,
I only feel my lack,
I doubt that I can even get,
Through this week intact.

I doubt that I am different,
I doubt that I am the same,
I doubt that people like me,
When they hear my name.

I question that by tomorrow,
Today's happiness will be gone,
I doubt that I have the strength,
To no longer be forlorn.

I'm told to trust the Universe,
And all that's meant to be,
To trust in myself and others,
To attract good things to me.

I doubt it is so simple,
That a happy carefree life,
Starts with me simply trusting,
There's more out there than strife.

Day one, it seems to be working,
I'm trusting more and more,
I ask the Universe for something,
And it opens up a door.

I doubt it will keep happening,
Surely soon my luck will slow,
I doubt in myself so much,
That's all I seem to know.

Day two, I'm still improving,
Despite such lack of belief,
Saying the words with confidence,
Has swept away some grief.

I'm feeling much more certain,
It's just as I was told,
Trust in the energy you project,
And for sure great things unfold.

subtle

HARBOUR MASTER

(Divine Intervention)

Why me?
Stormy sea,
Anchor dragging
My boat free.

Harbour master,
Get here faster,
Please help,
Save and grasp her.

I'm sitting thinking,
We're not sinking,
My fear now,
Slowly shrinking.

Help dispatched,
Rope attached,
Harbour master,
Did react.

feeling

SPIRITUAL JUNKIES

Spiritual Junkies everywhere,
Driving their camper van tyres bare,
Collecting crystals, braiding their hair,
Stories of awakening are quick to share.

Too much chat and not much quiet,
Fair trade coffee is their diet,
Talk of energy from the sun,
And how bliss awaits everyone.

Some are close but not quite there,
They hide this feeling of despair,
Unable to see through their third eye,
So perplexed, they don't know why.

The answer is to drop their act,
Connection's there with increased tact,
Clarity revealed without the fumble,
Spiritual power only to the humble.

easy

SPACE-PART 1

When you gaze up at the
sky in contemplation,
So much deep space for
human consideration,
Even with a telescope the
'Particle Horizon' is,
A glimpse of what's out
there and actually exists.

Vast distances of scale
impossible to conceive,
Astronomical measurements
too difficult to perceive,
Cosmic landmarks we have
heard of and are aware,
So hard to mentally picture
what's floating around up there.

To get a sense of scale: our
planets cloud base is,
Two thousand feet or
point six kilometers,
An airplane flies at ten
kilometers, for reference, and
Forty thousand kilometers is
our earth's circumference.

First up, the 'Karman Line'
marking the start of outer space,
Is located a hundred kilometers
from planet earth's face,

The International Space Station
sits in this cosmic fairway,
Is three hundred and fifty
kilometers from our earth away.

Three hundred and eighty thousand
kilometers from the 'I.S.S',
Sits our remarkable moon in all
its glorious white brightness,
Then there's a huge jump
to the planet nearest us,
Forty million kilometers away
is sulfuric coated Venus.

One hundred and fifty million
kilometers from us is our sun,
With its four million kilometer
circumference warming everyone,
And forty trillion kilometers
from us is the next nearest star,
Proxima Centauri, one-
seventh our sun's diameter.

Where is the 'edge of the
Universe' demarcation?
Forty six light years away
is the latest calculation,
A light year equates to ten
trillion kilometers, they say,
So, times that by forty-six
and that's how far away!

to

SPACE-PART 2

continued

Tucked in amongst all the stars,
planets and galaxies are,
Ninety-six percent of the Universe:
dark energy and dark matter,
Entirely unknown and mysterious
to all the astrophysicists,
Who despite their best efforts
can't make any sense of this.

Within this mix according to
the String Theory mould,
Eleven dimensions explained
by the Calabi-Yau Manifold,
Infinite possibilities well beyond
our realm of thinking,
A space so colossal and yet
curiously interlinking.

dismiss,

FINDING WITHIN-PART 1

What's the deal this going within,
How to start and where to begin,
I've been told it takes
lots of discipline,
Years to cultivate and
lots of meditating.

I go to yoga nearly every day,
We end each session
with "Namaste",
We close our eyes and pray
with raised hands,
The meaning of which
none of us understands.

I've heard to be any
good at it, there's a
crossed legged position
in which to sit,
You must fast, and purify,
not drink alcohol,
Chant a transcendental
mantra to your soul.

You must deny yourself
any carnal pleasure,
Give to the poor everything
you treasure,
And only then can you
have a good go,
With true commitment you
might feel some flow.

I've been told to stare
at a candle flame,
To eliminate every
thought is the aim,
To maintain this state is
very hard for me,
A few seconds I manage
occasionally.

I've got books, phone apps,
and CD's aplenty,
I've attempted to follow
and failed so miserably,
Each states a few simple
steps to follow,
The more I fail, the more
I'm left hollow.

I bought lots of crystals,
even set up a grid,
To raise my vibration,
open my third eyelid,
But I don't think it's really
done any good,
My vibration doesn't feel
as high as it should.

I'm feeling tired and
dragging my feet,
Perplexed, overwhelmed
in a state of defeat,

Once

FINDING WITHIN-PART 2
continued

In yoga classes during the
breathing technique,
My exhaustion take over
and I just fall asleep.

Then out of the blue I
tried a reiki session,
I was curious after a
friend's suggestion,
The room was calm, a
sensation of peace,
And within seconds I felt
my tension decrease.

The Reiki Master touched
my feet and my toes,
I felt an energy enter me from
where, heaven knows,
The room seemed to buzz,
I felt safe and warm,
And the edges of my body
seemed to lose all form.

I felt an expansion from
very deep within,
I became part of, well, ...
everything,
An all-encompassing
powerful connection,
A very familiar loving
cosmic re-union.

A memory surfacing, of
this elusive state,
The tools now remembered
how to meditate,
Not possible to learn from
any books you are reading,
You have to feel the very essence
of what you're achieving.

The space in between the
thoughts is where the power is,
That's the silence you are
trying to access and harness,
It's not about blocking all
thoughts, but to let them flow,
To have no attachment, let
them freely come and go.

So, that's what the deal is,
the 'finding within,'
A connection to one-ness is
what you're embracing,
A path that once discovered
really talks to your Soul,
Meditation is the gateway to
become part of the whole.

connected

EXPECTATIONS

Nothing is expected of us
Whilst we're on this earthly sphere,
Except to experience life fully
As a human whilst we are here.

Then slowly start remembering
Our true spiritual course
And prepare for our return
Re-uniting back with Source.

though

FOREVER PRESENT

An ice cube has definite form,
Tangible matter visibly there,
Then it melts and evaporates,
It still exists but now as air.

hard

LEMONGRASS

(Discovering Higher Self)

Lemongrass, we're newly acquainted,
Such a beautiful flavour and scent,
You're so pure, so fresh and untainted,
Bland food now so magnificent.

I've heard you spoken of so highly,
An ingredient I just couldn't see,
You're part of my cooking everyday now,
Finally liberated from imposed dormancy.

to

A DOG'S UNDERSTANDING

My dog seems to understand,
With no opposable thumb on his hand,
That living in the now is true bliss,
No future or past does he desire or miss.

Homo sapiens evolved the more advanced,
Problem solving much more enhanced,
They domesticated dogs to raise the alarm,
Protecting their camps from outside harm.

The dogs have now become our pets,
A safe walled garden keeps out the threats,
Food and water supplied routinely,
Allows the dog to exist serenely.

We're consumed with our working day,
Whilst our dog's at home engaged in play,
He chases butterflies and lays in the sun,
He is never bored with his sense of fun.

His happiness comes from no hurry,
A place of calm devoid of worry,
True contentment, he needs nothing more,
All achieved without a thumb on his paw!

miss,

FAMILIAR STRANGERS

Inwardly thank everyone
you have ever met,
Some people stand out,
some you forget,
But their energy is shared,
forever intertwined,
Your life is a million
moments combined.

Life lessons that you have
gratefully absorbed,
Even all the ones you
stubbornly ignored,
Many traits came from
these people originally,
Incorporated in your actions
now, so distinctly.

You're a conduit carrying part
of their life's intention,
When you quote them, it's
as if they're in the room,
Realise that any differences
are simply for polarity,
Because of them you have grown
and gained more clarity.

There is so much to value,
to love and hold dear,
Experience from the lessons
found in love and fear,
Assisted by familiar strangers,
you feel you know,
Your soul family down
here helping you grow.

As

EGO

Ego forms when you are ten,
Impressive armour to hide within,
You share your true self with very few,
A bolder image now friends accrue.

Then you're stuck with this act,
Your ego now established fact,
But you wear it so self-assured,
Suppressing the shame of being a fraud.

You practise this for forty years,
Learn to hide from all your fears,
Eventually become sick of the game,
And search for your true self again.

To re-acquaint takes quite some time,
To be authentic and feel fine,
Decades wasted whilst you grew,
Caring what others thought of you.

Other people wear this disguise too,
So self-absorbed, was oblivious to you,
But not too late to see the light,
To view the world without such fright.

Now confidence driven from within,
At last, your true growth can begin,
A fresh start with a subtle déjà vu,
And wisdom here to now assist you.

it

A COW LIVING IN THE NOW

A cow stands in her field,
Chewing on grass and hay,
With not much to do,
Therefore, not much to say.

But so happy in her field,
No desires of grasses greener,
No concerns of captivity,
Or, an open gate to free her.

She lifts her head up from a patch,
In order to survey,
What other clump of greenery,
She might move onto that day.

She relocates about three steps,
Inspired by this fresh cluster,
Keeps this routine for a year,
Until the day of muster.

Head lifted high and curious,
What's that noise occurring?
Unknown sounds of helicopters
Approaching engines whirring.

Truly startled she takes flight,
Calm grass eating days are over,
Actually and metaphorically,
She's forced off her patch of clover.

There is a point to this story,
Our cow was content and calm,
Until one day an external force,
Imposed great threat and harm.

Enjoy 'the now' like our cow,
Content in the field she did saunter,
As life is such that you can't predict,
How much your plans might alter!

will

MOSQUITO

A mosquito is my greatest hate,
However that has changed of late,
I observed under a magnifier,
This little blood-sucking vampire.

She is in fact full of beauty,
Equipped to go about her duty,
Segmented legs long and fine,
An immense length to her spine.

Her fine probus can generate,
Enough strength to penetrate,
Our thick skin has no defences,
When her feeding time commences.

Close up her head's endearing,
Antennae represent her hearing,
Multiple sections to her eye,
Wing structure of a dragonfly.

She is covered in ciliary hair,
And armour protected hardware,
Magnified in this much detail,
She is tough, certainly not frail.

Mother Nature made her perfect,
An insect perhaps to respect,
Her job here unknown to us,
Maybe not so superfluous.

Think when one next annoys you,
She's made up of stardust too,
Part of the consciousness whole,
A living entity perhaps with a soul.

fill

LADY ON THE BEACH

I am with my dog on the beach,
Approaching me a lady walking,
She moves with a slight lazy foot,
When she nears she and I start talking.

What an engaging lovely smile,
A short conversation we share,
As she turns away from me,
I see a fresh scar within her hair.

What has she recently endured?
A dozen stitches so matter of fact,
Was it painful or life threatening?
I never did see her again after that.

When a stranger briefly chats to you,
For that very short time together,
Your life's path is intertwined too,
A subtle energy in the ether forever.

you

PERSPECTIVE

A grain of sand,
In your hand,
To atoms and quarks,
An entire mass of land.

Astronauts in space,
Can't see your face,
Consider all scale,
From the viewers place.

A teeny bug in a flower,
His kingdom grand,
All he needs there,
His Holy land.

That's his divinity,
Needs no theology,
Life for him,
Is not a big mystery.

Define our nirvana,
With such simplicity,
A place of perfection,
And natural harmony.

Perhaps it's before us,
In our vicinity,
In fact far too obvious,
To plainly see.

It's the air we breathe,
And the life giving sun,
It's the crystal clear water,
And enchanted bird song.

No search required,
Perspective is the key,
Focus on all you can
Feel, hear and see.

with

SAFE HOLDING

See every occasion,
As potential unfolding,
A miraculous happening,
Released from safe holding.

pure

FLIP FLOP

(The Cycle Of Life)

A lone flip flop,
Washed up on the beach,
Salty and sandy,
And UV bleached.

Perma-shaped now,
The heel left its dent,
Wear and tear from
All the places it went.

So well worn,
Once part of a pair,
But now separated,
Past the point of repair.

The end of its journey,
Attached to some lad,
A story embedded,
Of the fun life it had.

Breaking down slowly,
By the waters motion,
Its billion atoms now
Part of the ocean.

bliss.

ANTS ON A ROPE

The standard accepted model is,
Humans view the world in 4D,
3D space and one 1D time,
Ideal for what we need.

In nineteen-nineteen Kaluza said,
5D exists as the maths says so,
An entrance smaller than an atom,
Hidden within the 4D
world we know.

Then 'Superstring' theory
claimed 10D,
And 'Membrane' theory
another more,
In fact, there's infinite variations,
That the scientists are
keen to explore.

The entrances to these realms,
Are mostly sub atomic in size,
Humans aren't conditioned
to see them,

And yet they're right
before our eyes.

Science describes a hidden existence,
Using the 'ants on a rope' analogy,
The ants are invisible
to us from afar,
With the rope seen as
a thin line in 1D.

The presence of hidden layers,
Explains why gravity on
earth is so weak,
Subtle openings into
these dimensions,
Is where our gravity is said to leak.

How to summarise the Cosmos:
An infinitely layered tapestry,
With a weave of vibrating
radiant light,
And a living consciousness
called 'Source Energy'.

Printed and bound by PG in the USA

USA2019PGIL